Published by Humble Creek, P.O. Box 719, Uhrichsville, Ohio 44683

Printed in China.
5 4 3 2 1

Happy Mother's Day

ELLYN SANNA

HUMBLECREEK
INSPIRATION FOR LIFE

Happy Mother's Day.
You are loved every day,
which means that
every day is Mother's Day!

Maternal love:
a miraculous substance
which God multiplies
as He divides it.

VICTOR HUGO

Thank you for your love, Mother.
You'll always have mine in return.

1

Memories of You

My Mother's Hands

Hands of love. . .
Began each day folded in prayer.
Opened to receive me when I hurt.
Held my favorite storybook and turned the pages.
Baked a cake for my special day each year.
Brushed away my tears.
Cradled my head when I was sick.
Clapped for me with encouragement and praise.
Reached out to others.
Cared for our house, making it a home.
Waved good-bye as I left that home.
And did so much more before. . .
At the end of each day, they folded again in prayer.

*Y*our smile always made me happy.

A glad heart makes a happy face.

PROVERBS 15:13 NLT

*M*y life as it is today stands on a foundation of memory.
Thank you for the firm foundation you gave me.
Thank you for all my memories of you.

2

Your Words
of Wisdom

Over the years, my view of you has changed.

- When I was four, I thought,
  My mommy knows everything!

- When I was eight, I said,
  My mom knows a lot! A whole lot!

- By the time I was twelve, I was thinking,
  My mother doesn't know everything after all.

- At fourteen, I thought,
  Of course my mother doesn't know that either.

- When I was sixteen, I decided,
  My mother is totally old-fashioned.

- ·By eighteen, I'm afraid I sometimes thought,
  That old woman? She doesn't know anything.

- But by the time I was twenty-five, I was thinking,
  Well, Mother might know something about life after all.

And now. . .well, as an adult, I'm so grateful for all the years you've shared your ideas with me.

I treasure your wisdom.

13

My Mother's Favorite Sayings

When you find yourself in a hole. . .
stop digging.

When you point a finger at someone else,
remember four more are pointing back at you.

It's not what we eat that matters,
but who we eat with.

The will of God will not take you where
the grace of God cannot keep you.

Each day, say "I love you" at least once.
Each day with God's help live your "I love you's."

When God's children are in need,
you be the one to help them out.

Learn something new every day.

*S*ome of the questions you asked I never quite understood.
Then I became a mother. . .
and I found myself asking the very same questions:

• "Who do you think you are?"

• "Do you think money grows on trees?"

• "If everyone jumped off a bridge, would you?"

- "Do you know how late it is?"

- "What were you thinking?"

    When I hear my voice ask your old questions,
    I have to smile.
    One day do you think my children
    will ask *their* children the very same things?

Lessons from My Mother

God will be with you when you. . .
Stand for what is right.
Speak in kindness.
Share with others.

God will help you to. . .
Open your eyes to His world.
Open your hands to His children.
Open your ears to hear cries for help.
Open your heart to His love.

If you do these things. . .
Your heart will be full.
Your life will have meaning.
That's what my mother taught me.

God pardons like a mother
who kisses the offense into everlasting forgetfulness.

HENRY WARD BEECHER

Thank you, Mother, for teaching me how to forgive.
Perhaps even more important—you taught me to ask for forgiveness.
You spoke these lessons without a word.
You simply lived them.

Remember, the Lord forgave you,
so you must forgive others.

COLOSSIANS 3:13 NLT

*A mother's love is indeed the golden link that binds youth to age;
and he is still but a child, however time may have furrowed his cheek,
or silvered his brow, who can yet recall, with a softened heart,
the fond devotion, or the gentle chidings of
the best friend that God ever gave us.*

CHRISTIAN NESTELL BOVEE

*No matter my age, Mother,
I'm glad I'll always be your child . . .
and I'll never be too old to benefit from your wisdom.*

3

Your Legacy

You gave me a legacy. . .
one of character, strength, and faith. . .
a legacy of more value than any other inheritance
you could have given me.

The LORD is my chosen portion

and my cup; you hold my lot.

The boundary lines have

fallen for me in pleasant places;

I have a goodly heritage.

PSALM 16:5–6 NRSV

As Jesus and the disciples continued on their way to Jerusalem, they came to a village where a woman named Martha welcomed them into her home. Her sister, Mary, sat at the Lord's feet, listening to what he taught. But Martha was worrying over the big dinner she was preparing. She came to Jesus and said, "Lord, doesn't it seem unfair to you that my sister just sits here while I do all the work? Tell her to come and help me."

But the Lord said to her, "My dear Martha, you are so upset over all these details! There is really only one thing worth being concerned about. Mary has discovered it—and I won't take it away from her."

LUKE 10:38–42 NLT

Mother, I have watched you balance the attributes of both a Mary and a Martha in your life. Your Martha qualities—years of commitment and service to your family, community, and church—never overpowered your Mary's heart. Somehow, through all the busy years, you found time for reflection, prayer, and waiting on the presence of God.

In my own busy life today, I strive to imitate your Martha-dedication and Mary-serenity. Sometimes, the two sisters seem to quarrel in my heart. Thank you for showing me that their two natures can actually complement one another. Your example is my legacy of hope.

A Gentle Gardener

You acted as a gardener in my life.
You planted seeds of love, joy, and curiosity.
You nourished them with caring, wisdom, and faith.
Sometimes you needed to weed and prune the garden.
I never liked that much.
But your encouragement and praise made me blossom.
Through the changing seasons of my life,
you have worked with the Master Gardener,
to help me grow.
And now I share my harvest with the world.

4

My Gratitude

Once we were simply mother and child.
That hasn't changed,
but now we have become even more.
Now we are friends.
I'm glad!

Her children rise up and call her blessed.

PROVERBS 31:28 RSV

*C*harm is deceptive, and beauty is fleeting;
but a woman who fears the LORD is to be praised.

PROVERBS 31:30 NIV

The Carousel

Our relationship, that of mother and child, is like a carousel.
The carousel turns, and the scene changes. . .
just as our relationship has changed.

I look forward to each new turn,
for with each new cycle in our lives,
I learn more about you. . .
and more about myself, as well.

Your Strength

When things have gone wrong in my life,
I know you always wish you could take my pain
and bear it instead of me.
You can't do that, of course.
But you have done something even better. . .
You have stood beside me, offering me your strength.
Thank you.